MW00761037

*Twelve Angels and*
*Cherubs Bookmarks*

**DOVER PUBLICATIONS**

*Twelve Angels and*
*Cherubs Bookmarks*

**DOVER PUBLICATIONS**

*Twelve Angels and
Cherubs Bookmarks*

DOVER PUBLICATIONS

*Twelve Angels and
Cherubs Bookmarks*

DOVER PUBLICATIONS

*Twelve Angels and
Cherubs Bookmarks*

**DOVER PUBLICATIONS**

*Twelve Angels and
Cherubs Bookmarks*

**DOVER PUBLICATIONS**

*Twelve Angels and
Cherubs Bookmarks*

**DOVER PUBLICATIONS**

*Twelve Angels and
Cherubs Bookmarks*

**DOVER PUBLICATIONS**

*Twelve Angels and
Cherubs Bookmarks*

**DOVER PUBLICATIONS**

*Twelve Angels and
Cherubs Bookmarks*

**DOVER PUBLICATIONS**

*Twelve Angels and
Cherubs Bookmarks*

DOVER PUBLICATIONS

*Twelve Angels and
Cherubs Bookmarks*

DOVER PUBLICATIONS